A Reflective PLANNING JOURNAL for SCHOOL LEADERS

With thanks and admiration—
This book is dedicated to Mc Blasdell, Steve Davenport, and
John Sido—three extraordinary mentors, friends, and role models.

A Reflective PLANNING JOURNAL for SCHOOL LEADERS

With Insights and Tips From Award-Winning Principals

Olaf Jorgenson

For information:

Corwin Press
A SAGE Company
2455 Teller Road
Thousand Oaks, California 91320
www.corwinpress.com

SAGE India Pvt. Ltd.
B 1/I 1 Mohan Cooperative
Industrial Area
Mathura Road, New Delhi 110 044
India

SAGE Ltd.
1 Oliver's Yard
55 City Road
London EC1Y 1SP
United Kingdom

SAGE Asia-Pacific Pte. Ltd.
33 Pekin Street #02-01
Far East Square
Singapore 048763

Printed in the United States of America

Library of Congress Cataloging-in-Publication Data

Jorgenson, Olaf.
A reflective planning journal for school leaders : with insights and tips from award-winning principals / Olaf Jorgenson.
p. cm.
ISBN 978-1-4129-5808-0 (cloth)
ISBN 978-1-4129-5809-7 (pbk.)
1. School management and organization—United States. 2. Schedules, School—United States. I. Title.

LB2805.R67 2008
371.2'07—dc22 2008001245

This book is printed on acid-free paper.

08 09 10 11 12 10 9 8 7 6 5 4 3 2 1

Acquisitions Editor: Arnis Burvikovs
Editorial Assistants: Irina Dragut and Ena Rosen
Production Editor: Veronica Stapleton
Copy Editor: Edward Meidenbauer
Typesetter: C&M Digitals (P) Ltd.
Proofreader: Dennis W. Webb
Cover Designer: Karine Hovsepian

Contents

Preface

Effective school leaders are learners first. Yet few of us make time every day for reflection and professional growth, particularly in the critical first few years of our tenures as principals, when many of our workday habits take hold. In part, that's because we feel the pressures of time and our expansive commitments, often compounded by the weight of emergencies and the incessant barrage of immediate demands that are inevitable aspects of our role.

Regular use of the Journal is intended to help school leaders develop the practice of reflection—which, given principals' harried schedules, must be deliberately incorporated into their daily and weekly routine. The isolation of the principalship, paired with the constant shortage of time, makes it difficult for school leaders to engage in ongoing professional development or to find convenient access to helpful suggestions from peers or from the research. The Journal is meant as a functional way for principals to begin addressing this problem, building or extending their leadership repertoires. I also hope that the Journal will be used by superintendents and district office leaders as they mentor the principals in their charge.

HOW IS THE JOURNAL DESIGNED TO WORK?

Each month the reflective calendar carries a theme relating to the tasks and events common to that month of the principal's year: Startup activities in August and September, teacher evaluation and testing in the spring months, a mix of planning and self-renewal in the summer, and more. (Some principals whose schools operate on a nontraditional schedule will have to adapt the Journal's planner features to fit the rhythm of their calendar.) For each week, readers will find inspirational quotes that reinforce hopeful attitudes toward schooling and leadership, also useful for the principal's newsletter or to set the tone in a faculty meeting. Weekly questions serve as prompts for reflection and journaling. And at the core of the Journal are insights and tips from award-winning elementary, middle, and high school principals, corresponding to the monthly calendar themes.

The Resources section at the end of the book provides additional observations of special interest to prospective or beginning school leaders, mostly gleaned from my own experience in public, private, and international schools over the past two decades.

THE VALUE—AND POWER—OF REFLECTION

Reflection can rejuvenate, inspire, realign; we've all seen teachers who engage in reflective practices, like career ladder programs and National Board Certification, and subsequently exhibit significantly improved professionalism, resourcefulness, engagement, leadership, and even attitudes. The same can be true for principals, as we strive to be proactive rather than reactive leaders, more aware of our aims and motivations and eager to learn better ways of accomplishing our objectives.

The practice of self-evaluation is integral to effective leadership in any organization, but particularly in schools because of the highly affective context of schooling—schools are more like families than businesses, and the emphasis on relationships can make executive functions such as conflict resolution more complex. Overcoming the difficult situations that present themselves in school leadership demands that we make time to actively assess the circumstances as soon as possible, evaluating and planning ahead, taking control rather than being swept along by undercurrents of emotion and competing demands that overtake the best-planned days. Often there seems no time to make time, and consequently we can rush decisions that we discover in hindsight would have been well served by pause and more deliberate analysis.

Even if this means carving out five minutes before turning out the lights and heading home in the evening, or considering reflective questions on the drive to or from work each day, there is always time if the process of reflection is important enough. Veteran school leaders I know have learned to make time to process, evaluate, regroup; and to an individual, they consider it vital in their continuing success and growth in the long term. Immediately, the regular practice of reflection helps principals clarify assumptions and regain or maintain a big-picture perspective, moving them toward more strategic and less reactive decision making.

MAKING REFLECTION WORK FOR YOU

Reflection is useful only if it is applied. Creating time to evaluate one's progress, take stock of challenges and resources, and "return to the balcony" enables refocusing on long-term goals that are otherwise obscured by day-to-day management pressures. All are healthy outcomes of using a deliberate planning tool like this Journal. You might emerge from your work in the Journal with great ideas, but you need to enlist your staff and broader support network to implement them. Consequently, you'll note that many of the reflective questions direct you to consider how you'll engage teachers and colleagues in support of your long-term objectives, which requires dialogue and motivation. (For those of you using the Journal in a mentoring context, the questions provide a mechanism to move from reflection, to brainstorming and sharing, to strategy.)

We all acknowledge that immediate pressures demand a school leader's attention and squeeze time for reflection to a minimum. High-stakes testing, heightened accountability pressures, and increasing competition between and among public, charter, independent, and parochial schools (and home schooling) form an ever-present backdrop to the principal's experience today. Our day-to-day lives can be determined by the constant, unpredictable, unscheduled problems and issues that arise, from facilities concerns like leaking roofs and faltering sound systems and plumbing hassles, to student conduct issues, staff emergencies, personal and health-related issues, and more. Stress, ambiguity, and unpredictability are ever-present aspects of the principal's daily experience that can threaten even the best intentions for reflective thinking and planning.

This is precisely why reflection is crucial for principals who strive to do more than manage external demands; reflection can serve to help school leaders keep a perspective on the scope of their responsibilities beyond today's laser focus on outcomes, and look up and out into the future of the schools they hope to create and serve.

This underscores why *A Reflective Planning Journal for School Leaders* is a valuable resource, because using it regularly, especially in a peer partnership or mentoring relationship, can enable school leaders to make reflective practice a habit. As with so many choices and priorities school leaders must define, we have to *make time* for reflection if we recognize its benefits and believe it's important enough. It certainly has improved my practice and my perspectives on my work as it relates to my values, my own growth as a leader, and the big-picture goals I've set for my school. I sincerely hope new and seasoned principals find the Journal useful as a practical tool for personal and professional development that can help them model—and benefit from—constant learning and growth.

Acknowledgments

During my career as an educator and school leader, I've relied on the talents and resourcefulness of people around me to inform and improve my efforts. The same is true when I write!

For this project, I extend my thanks to Tim Moe, a former colleague and a talented principal in the Mesa Public Schools, Arizona, who helped me get started. Doug Llewellyn, a friend and accomplished science educator and author, pointed me toward Corwin Press, whose mission *("Helping Educators Do Their Work Better")* matches my own motivation for writing. Dale Cox and Christopher Peal, principals and friends who reviewed and endorsed the book's concept, provided encouragement to complete the manuscript for publication with Corwin Press.

I owe a significant debt of gratitude to Mary McGrath, Beverly Johns, Joyce Kaser, Susan Mundry, Katherine Stiles, and the late Susan Loucks-Horsley, Corwin Press authors whose work helped inspire *A Reflective Planning Journal for School Leaders.*

I'd like to acknowledge the National Association of Elementary School Principals (NAESP) and the National Association of Secondary School Principals (NASSP), whose helpful staff members provided me access to their association databases, enabling me to solicit ideas and tips directly from the master principals recognized state-by-state each year. I hope this book honors their prestigious school leader award programs:

- *NAESP National Distinguished Principals:* Established in 1984, this program honors exemplary elementary and middle school principals who "set the pace, character, and quality of the education children receive during their early school years." The program is sponsored by NAESP in cooperation with the U.S. Department of Education, supported by a corporate partnership with AIG VALIC.

- *NAESP Peer Assisted Leadership Services (PALS):* NAESP created the PALS Corps in collaboration with Nova Southeastern University to provide the first national mentoring certification for principal mentors. PALS participants are experienced school leaders trained and accredited to serve as peer mentors for new and aspiring principals.

• *NASSP/MetLife Principals of the Year:* This program began in 1993 to recognize outstanding middle level and high school principals. The program honors secondary school principals "who have succeeded in providing high-quality learning opportunities for students as well as exemplary contributions to the profession."

Above all, I am indebted to the extraordinary school leaders who volunteered their ideas and suggestions that constitute the core of this book:

Pam N. Bradley, 2005 NAESP Distinguished Principal, Muskogee 7th & 8th Grade Center, Muskogee, OK

Tom Burton, 2006 NASSP/MetLife Principal of the Year, Cuyahoga Heights Middle School, Cuyahoga Heights, OH

Sharon Byrdsong, 2005 NASSP/MetLife Principal of the Year, Azalea Gardens Middle School, Norfolk, VA

Steve Clarke, 2005 NASSP/MetLife Principal of the Year, Bellingham High School, Bellingham, WA

Maria Corso, 2005 NAESP Distinguished Principal, Lyncrest School, Fair Lawn, NJ

Jim Elefante, 2006 NASSP/MetLife Principal of the Year, Londonderry High School, Londonderry, NH

Nancy Gregory, 2006 NASSP/MetLife Principal of the Year, Blythewood Middle School, Blythewood, SC

Bruce Haddix, 2005 NAESP Distinguished Principal, Center Grove Elementary School, Greenwood, IN

Dick Jones, 2006 NASSP/MetLife Principal of the Year, John Adams Middle School, Rochester, MN

Melissa Klopfer, 2005 NAESP Distinguished Principal, Aviano Elementary School, Department of Defense Education Activity (DoDEA), Italy

Gary Lester, 2006 NASSP/MetLife Principal of the Year, Thornwood High School, South Holland, IL

Brian McQueen, 2005 NAESP Distinguished Principal, Westmoreland Road Elementary School, Whitesboro, NY

David Montague, 2005 NAESP Distinguished Principal, Washington Elementary School, Kennewick, WA

Sarah Peoples Perry, 2006 NAESP PALS Principal, Campostella Elementary School of Excellence, Norfolk, VA

Melinda Reeves, 2004 NASSP/MetLife Principal of the Year, Decatur High School, Decatur, TX

Mike Scott, 2004 NASSP/MetLife Principal of the Year, Poynter Middle School, Hillsboro, OR

Suzanne E. Smith, 2005 NAESP Distinguished Principal, Gertrude Walker Elementary School, Garden City, KS

Ronna Steel, 2006 NASSP/MetLife Principal of the Year, Union City Middle School, Union City, MI

Linda Stroud, 2005 NASSP/MetLife Principal of the Year, Greeneville Middle School, Greeneville, TN

Todd Wolverton, 2005 NASSP/MetLife Principal of the Year, Creston High School, Creston, IA

Sandra Jo-Anne Young, 2006 NASSP/MetLife Principal of the Year, Kamehameha Middle School, Kapalama Campus, Honolulu, HI

Finally, I appreciate the skillful, upbeat, and considerate work of Corwin Press's editorial team, especially Hudson Perigo, Lizzie Brenkus, Rachel Livsey, Arnis Burvikovs, Edward Meidenbauer, and Veronica Stapleton, whose guidance and encouragement led to substantial improvements and, I hope, a final product that will be useful for the practitioners this book is intended to support.

Thank you, everyone!

PUBLISHER'S ACKNOWLEDGMENTS

Corwin Press gratefully acknowledges the contributions of the following reviewers:

Robert A. Frick
Superintendent of Schools
Lampeter-Strasburg School District
Lampeter, PA

Jeanine Heil
Assistant Principal
West Windsor-Plainsboro Regional School District
Princeton Junction, NJ

Scott Hollinger
Principal
IDEA Quest College Preparatory
McAllen, TX

Michelle L. Kocar
Principal
Heritage South Elementary School
Avon, OH

Tom Lickona
Professor of Education; Director, Center for the 4th and 5th Rs
State University of New York at Cortland
Cortland, NY

Mark A. Merrell
Principal
James Madison High School
Vienna, VA

Rick Miller
Superintendent
Oxnard School District
Oxnard, CA

Guylene Robertson
Superintendent of Schools
Goodrich, TX

About the Author

Olaf (Ole) Jorgenson has served as a teacher and school leader in a variety of public and independent schools in the United States and abroad over the past 20 years. His publications and conference presentations promote leadership strategies and instructional approaches to benefit practitioners. Currently, Ole is head of school-elect at Almaden Country School in San Jose, California, an independent PreK–eighth grade college preparatory school dedicated to "discovering the gifts in every child." Ole and his wife, Tanya, their daughter, Juliette, and Lucy the Dog make their home in San Jose. Ole enjoys consulting and collaborating on projects with other educators who seek to improve teaching and learning. He can be reached at olafjorgenson@yahoo.com.

August

Aspirations

Theme

Aspirations: Share your vision for the school and bring the staff together to set and promote your schoolwide goals and action plan

To Do

Communicate your vision for the school—one that encompasses what the school community *is,* and what it aspires to *become;* include schoolwide goals for the year ahead

Define and reiterate the school's core values and how colleagues will interact to reach shared objectives: What do we believe about teaching and learning?

Meet and orient new teachers, students, families

Plan for open house

Plan back-to-school meetings with staff

Prep for student registration and balance class loads; be prepared for scheduled and unscheduled meetings with parents

Other

___

___

Consider This: Insights and Tips From Award-Winning Principals

We review our school mission and belief statements together in August, before the students arrive. I ask the staff to "recall" our mission statement by using a "fill-in-the-blank" review to see how much they've internalized. It does no good to have a mission statement unless we can assimilate and verbalize to others what we are all about.

We also have a staff mini-retreat before school begins. We make it a point to go away somewhere—to a state park, or hotel with a meeting place—so we are together for 2–3 days and can talk all about school without interruptions. It's important to plan as much collegial team-building time as work time. I always make sure the accommodations are nice and the food is great to thank them for their hard work. I give them lots of shopping time and plan fun activities together in the evenings. This is an excellent way to help staff members get to know each other better, with no pressure to perform, especially the new teachers. We carefully analyze data from the previous year to set goals for the upcoming year. By the end of the retreat, we're all on the same page at the same time, right before school starts—it helps us be cohesive and collegial from day one.

—Bruce Haddix
2005 NAESP Distinguished Principal
Center Grove Elementary School, Greenwood, IN

When the teachers come back in August, my administrative team and I plan our special event for the first day of school—this day is the students' first impression of our school, and over the years, we've made it into a very memorable and fun experience for them. We welcome 320 new seventh graders each fall, and we want to make a lasting impact on their very first day in middle school. So, we host an assembly we call the "Kumu [Hawaiian for teacher or leader] on Parade." In this assembly on the first day of school, every adult who affects the life of the children in the coming year—teachers, custodial and maintenance staff, librarians, dining hall workers, secretaries, administrators—is introduced individually and walks once around our gymnasium, ending by taking a bow and receiving applause. This year even some of our board members and central office administrators participated. The first-day assembly culminates with all the adults joining together to do a dance. One of our teachers is a professional ballroom dancer and choreographs the dance, and we all spend a couple of days learning the steps before the first day. This year we had a western theme for the year, so we all did a line dance for the children, but every year it's something different and every year, we all have to learn a new dance! The assembly is a wonderful, positive way to start the year with a spirited welcome. High school students come back to the middle school and tell us they still remember the Kumu on Parade even after they graduate, with fond memories of being introduced to the adults who care about them, and then having all the adults performing a special dance expressly for them.

—Sandra Jo-Anne Young
2006 NASSP/MetLife Principal of the Year
Kamehameha Middle School, Kapalama Campus, Honolulu, HI

Hopefully, your hiring is finished by August, but occasionally you have a last-minute resignation or an opportunity for additional staffing. We do something a little different with hiring of teachers. We include students and parents on our hiring teams. When we have summer school classes in session, we ask teacher candidates to do mini-lessons in the summer program classes happening onsite. Then, we ask the students in the summer school to provide feedback on the quality of the candidates based on the actual lessons. During the year, you can do the same thing with your regular students. It's one thing to see a résumé and another to see a concept taught "live"—I've found it a very effective way to identify and hire excellent teachers.

—Melinda Reeves
2004 NASSP/MetLife Principal of the Year
Decatur High School, Decatur, TX

Weekly Inspirational Quotes for August

"Education is not the filling of a pail, but the lighting of a fire."

—W. B. Yeats

"There is no 'try.' Only 'do.'"

—Yoda

"Good is the enemy of great."

—Jim Collins

"Treat children as if they were what they should be, and you help them become what they are capable of becoming."

—Johann Wolfgang von Goethe

"Courage is being scared to death—and saddling up anyway."

—John Wayne

Weekly Reflective Questions for August

This month's theme centers on "aspirations." Looking ahead, where do you want your school to be—compared to where you left off in June—when the school year ahead comes to a close? What are three measurable schoolwide goals for the coming year? How will you know whether you're making progress toward these goals?

____

____

____

____

For some teachers and students, the start of school involves considerable anxiety. What do you do to identify and support those individuals in your school community for whom "saddling up" for the first days of school is a tremendous stressor?

____

____

____

____

One of the monthly quotes asserts that "good is the enemy of great." Sometimes it is difficult to push for excellence when influential members of your staff and faculty feel things are "good enough" as is. Who are these individuals on your faculty and staff? How will you motivate them?

____

____

____

____

List three new, creative, fun strategies for recognizing the accomplishments of your staff, school volunteers, and students, motivating them in the upcoming year.

____

____

____

How strong is the leadership team at your school? What uncertainties or needs do you and your administrative team have heading into this school year? How do you intend to address the concerns and support the needs?

September

Beginnings

Theme

Beginnings: Help new colleagues, students, and families assimilate into your school community; use the previous year's student and teacher data to set benchmarks and monitor progress

To Do

Informal "welcome back" staff social

Opening of school assembly

Open house

Analyze test data from previous year; disaggregate for various subgroups and identify which areas or standards need more emphasis

Review teacher evaluation data to identify individual areas of concern and any trends that need attention; communicate to appropriate audiences

Other

____

____

____

____

Consider This: Insights and Tips From Award-Winning Principals

It's important to take time to nurture staff members after the initial weeks of school are behind them. I like to do spontaneous ice cream sundae parties or popcorn parties to thank teachers and support staff. But along with the spontaneity, planning should be set by this time of year. I distribute a calendar with the schedule of staff meetings for the year (or at least the first semester), inservice trainings, grade-level and leadership team meetings, open house, parent forums (times that parents can meet with me to share questions or concerns), parent conferences, standardized testing, fire and emergency drills, etc. I prepare a series of calendars looking ahead at least two months to specific upcoming events, and incorporate this into my periodic staff bulletin so people know what's coming up soon. I always try to be proactive in planning, and encourage my teachers to do the same. I plan for a half-day of teacher release time for planning during September and January each year, using my professional day supply. Here, teachers have a short, scripted agenda to cover (testing, scores, remediation, grade-level-specific items, etc.) and the rest of the time to plan together on their own. I buy lunch, which the teachers appreciate!

—Bruce Haddix
2005 NAESP Distinguished Principal
Center Grove Elementary School, Greenwood, IN

Our school year begins in August, so by September we're already well into the race through the busy fall. I give my teachers a month to get settled into their routines, and to decide what they'll work on for professional development during the year. We have institutional and schoolwide goals set by our central office, and in June everyone who wants to participate in a leadership workshop collaborates to set our goal for the middle school division (which integrates with and supports the systemwide goals). So, in September teachers develop their personal goals and are asked to make sure they relate to the divisional and systemwide goals. Their individual goals are professional and personal—what the individual teacher wants to accomplish in an area of improvement that may have been identified with a principal, or focusing on a personal goal like making more time for exercise or a hobby. The goals are due in the third week of September; I go over them and if they look good, I just tell the teacher her or his goals are approved and to go ahead. If the goals need more work, I'll meet with the staff member individually to rework them. We revisit the goals throughout the year; in April, the staff members review their goals and write a self-assessment of their progress, and we meet at year's end to discuss the results.

—Sandra Jo-Anne Young
2006 NASSP/MetLife Principal of the Year
Kamehameha Middle School, Kapalama Campus, Honolulu, HI

We have Senior Retreat each year soon after school starts. This is a day set aside for serious preparation regarding life after high school, including everything they need to know about the SAT, ACT, scholarships, etc., and then some fun bonding time as a class. We invite the parents to attend with their seniors from 8 a.m. until noon. During this time, we distribute and review our "Senior Survival Guide," which covers topics like filling out financial aid forms; college applications and visits; and ACT/SAT, AP, and other testing requirements. We have a panel of college representatives, technical school representatives, military representatives, former students, business partners, and parents who give advice and answer questions. At noon we have a cookout and a forum with the principal, followed by a fun afternoon of activities that include waterslides and games in which students compete individually and as homeroom groups. Senior Retreat provides not only valuable information but a memorable experience that starts the year off with a serious focus and fun memories.

—Melinda Reeves
2004 NASSP/MetLife Principal of the Year
Decatur High School, Decatur, TX

Weekly Inspirational Quotes for September

"Many things can wait; the child cannot. Now is the time his bones are being formed, his mind is being developed. To him, we cannot say tomorrow; his name is today."

—Gabriela Mistral

"We have not inherited the world from our forefathers—we have borrowed it from our children."

—Kashmiri proverb

"I skate to where the puck is going to be, not to where it has been."

—Wayne Gretzky

"If we are to reach real peace in this world, we shall have to begin with the children."

—Mahatma Gandhi

"One must care about a world one will never see."

—Bertrand Russell

Weekly Reflective Questions for September

This month's theme is "beginnings." Considering your annual schoolwide goals, what can you do *now* to contribute to successfully accomplishing what you've envisioned? In particular, how will you persuade colleagues to buy into your goals, especially those who are reluctant to support them?

____

____

____

____

How do your goals for this year support your long-range plan for the school over the next 3–5 years?

____

____

____

____

The quotation from Wayne Gretzky encourages us to be forward-looking. How do you balance a healthy respect for the school's traditions and accomplishments in the past, with the emerging needs and expectations to which it must adapt in the future?

____

____

____

____

Master principals, such as the three individuals whose suggestions are featured this month, are deliberate about celebrating and commemorating the beginning of the school year, capitalizing on the anticipation and energy students and staff bring back from summer break. What will you do to maintain the momentum established in the startup celebrations throughout the rest of the school year, especially when you get to the "doldrums" of February?

____

____

____

____

What systems do you have in place to monitor your new teachers, especially those in their first years in the profession? What special, intentional support structure do you have in place, such as peer mentoring, new teacher discussion groups, regularly scheduled social outings in the community, parent association "welcome baskets" and "care packages," or your own scheduled engagement with the new colleagues, throughout the school year to maximize the likelihood that the new teachers will assimilate and enjoy long tenures at your school? What resources can you tap to learn about what other principals are doing for their new teachers?

____

____

____

____

October

Community Building

Theme

Community building: Use parent conferences, PTA, open house, and principal-to-parent, student, and teacher forums to build relationships and develop community support for your schoolwide goals

To Do

Plan for parent conferences with the goal of reaching 100% of parents

Begin evaluation preconferences and schedule formal observations

Fall testing (where applicable)

Monitor new teacher progress and assimilation into faculty

Conduct mid-quarter student–parent conferences

Other

____

____

____

____

____

Consider This: Insights and Tips From Award-Winning Principals

In October, once everyone's settled into a rhythm, be sure to begin collection of documentation for your teacher evaluations. This is the time of the year to take pictures and notes to include in the evaluations. I find it really useful to have illustrations that help me compare how they began the school year with how they operate during and at the end of the school year—and it can be a good motivator and reminder for the teachers, too!

—Sarah Peoples Perry
2006 NAESP PALS Principal
Campostella Elementary School of Excellence, Norfolk, VA

A great way to get your community involved in school is to start a parent breakfast. The old adage, "If you feed them, they will come," holds true. We provide some bagels, juice, coffee, etc., and relay information about the good news and future projects going on in our school. I allow for open and honest feedback and remind myself not to be afraid to open up for dialogue. Far too often, administrators and teachers do not communicate with parents for fear of a disagreement. I think it's vital to listen first and share my point of view only after I've really heard what's being said. After all, we're all adults and at a minimum, we should be able to agree to disagree.

—Tom Burton
2006 NASSP/MetLife Principal of the Year
Cuyahoga Heights Middle School, Cuyahoga Heights, OH

We host "Parent University" classes in the evenings in our building. Session topics include anything from "Learning to Surf the Internet," to "Tips for Parents of Teens," to "Strategies for Applying for College and Completing Financial Aid Forms." Classes are comprised of one to four sessions. Our teachers provide the classes for nominal stipends, and parents love to attend the "university" for parents in their children's school.

We also send performance groups (choir, band, drama, etc.) to local retirement homes, town meetings, local churches, etc., prior to the holiday rush. The performers have usually had enough time to practice by this time of the year, and it's a wonderful experience for the students and their audiences—while providing great community relations for the school.

—Gary Lester
2006 NASSP/MetLife Principal of the Year
Thornwood High School, South Holland, IL

Weekly Inspirational Quotes for October

"None of us is as smart as all of us."

—Ken Blanchard

"The single biggest problem in communication is the illusion that it has taken place."

—Albert Einstein

"Teams, not individuals, are the fundamental learning unit in modern organizations . . . Unless teams can learn, the organization cannot learn."

—Peter Senge

"Either we're pulling together or we're pulling apart. Coming together is a beginning. Keeping together is progress. Working together is success."

—Henry Ford

"Do you want a collection of brilliant minds or a brilliant collection of minds?"

—R. Meredith Belbin

Weekly Reflective Questions for October

What does *community* mean to you? How would you rate the strength of your school's sense of community? What do you actively do to promote your school's mission and goals, strengthen the bonds within and between your various school constituencies, and develop a sense of unified purpose? What more would you like to do? How will you know one year from now that your efforts and new strategies are working?

____

____

____

____

At the heart of the process of building community are familiarity and relationships, which in turn rest on establishing and expanding a *network* of informed supporters. This is a monumental task for one person to accomplish. Whom do you enlist among your parent volunteers, PTSA members, students, teachers, and other staff to help you get your messages out, and to bring people together in support of shared goals?

____

____

____

____

Community building also rests on effective communication, and as Einstein suggests, often we assume communication is happening when it may not be. Much of the "communication" we generate is one-way, not providing for exchange of ideas or feedback. Consider your communication with your constituencies: How much of it is one-way (i.e., newsletters, e-bulletins, notes to parents, presentations or speeches, memoranda to staff)? How often do you provide meaningful interactive forums for brainstorming and gathering reactions and advice about your schoolwide goals with your constituents?

Some principals engage their staff during faculty meetings, soliciting expertise and making the periodic meetings opportunities for enrichment, recognition, and productive mutual sharing of ideas in a setting enlivened by food and music that fosters a sense of camaraderie and community. Often however, faculty meetings consist largely of delivering rather than exchanging information. How interactive are your meetings, and how much of what you cover could be appropriately delivered in a memorandum? Can you consult with peers and members of your staff to strengthen the dynamism, engagement, and community-building potential of your meetings?

One aspect of community building is developing (and demonstrating) pride in individual and group success. What do you do to communicate and recognize the accomplishments of your teachers and support staff members? Are you aware of creative recognition strategies fellow principals use to help build community in their schools?

November

Taking Stock

Theme

Taking stock: Look at the evidence of progress as the winter holidays near, and plan for adjustments where needed for the spring term

To Do

Analyze formative assessment data

Ensure that safety nets are in place for at-risk students and families

Conduct mid-year teacher observations and mid-year evaluation conferences

Plan winter events and shows

Other

Consider This: Insights and Tips From Award-Winning Principals

In November, we begin rehearsing for our staff Christmas show for the students—our staff members put together a holiday cabaret that we perform just for the kids and it has expanded each year into quite an extravaganza. This is our Christmas gift to the children and lets them see their teachers in a whole different light. Also, it really is a great activity for staff climate-building and cohesion—fun and nonthreatening.

—Bruce Haddix
2005 NAESP Distinguished Principal
Center Grove Elementary School, Greenwood, IN

How often do you visit classrooms outside of evaluations? If you have to think about the last time you visited a classroom, you are spending too much time on other things. The teachers are on the front lines and need to know that you care and that you know what is going on. Our initial commitment to being visible can fade at this busy time of year, so we need to be intentional about maintaining a presence.

—Tom Burton
2006 NASSP/MetLife Principal of the Year
Cuyahoga Heights Middle School, Cuyahoga Heights, OH

The key component, to make a real difference, is for teachers to analyze their *own* data from their *own* students that they have in their *own* classrooms each day! Then teachers will see the relevance and be more likely to adjust their instruction to meet student needs.

—Gary Lester
2006 NASSP/MetLife Principal of the Year
Thornwood High School, South Holland, IL

Weekly Inspirational Quotes for November

"Don't worry that children never listen to you. Worry that they are always watching you."

—Robert Fulghum

"Life is change. Growth is optional. Choose wisely."

—Karen Kaiser Clark

"Errors are portals of discovery."

—James Joyce

"It's amazing what can be accomplished when nobody cares who gets the credit."

—Tom Coughlin

"If you fall on your face, at least you're heading in the right direction."

—Bill O'Hanlan

Weekly Reflective Questions for November

"Life is change," as most people charged with leading organizations well understand. Considering members of your faculty who may be reluctant or resistant to change, how can you help them make adjustments based on mid-year achievement data? What is the source of their reluctance or resistance? Who among their peers can you enlist to assist you?

____

____

____

____

As you gather evidence of progress during the year with your various student and teacher initiatives—whether that takes the form of metrics like attendance records, achievement test scores, grades, and conduct marks, or less-quantifiable measures like the feel of the cafeteria at lunch, attendance at Friday teacher socials, and so forth—consider what success means to you at this time of year, and what you can do to enlist support toward increased success in the second term this year. What are the top three most important indicators of success at your school, and where do you want to be when you reflect again at the end of the year? One year from now?

____

____

____

____

The quotations by James Joyce and Bill O'Hanlan both speak to risk taking. How do you encourage seasoned teachers to try something new, or help your less-experienced teachers grow when their efforts and experiments fall short?

____

____

____

____

What do you do for those students, staff members, and families in your school community for whom the holidays are a difficult time, either as a consequence of poverty, personal illness, family problems, or other misfortune? How do you identify those within your school community who are in need at this time of year, and how might you incorporate student service to support such needs into your instructional program and co-curricular outreach efforts?

____

____

____

____

What celebrations does your school traditionally host to recognize the close of the calendar year and the various cultural holidays that accompany this time? Do you want to enrich your offerings and if so, what might be sources of information about how to honor the various ethnic, cultural, and religious traditions that exist in your school community? What are educational, creative, engaging ways to bring the community together in acknowledging your appreciation for its diversity and multicultural heritage during the holiday season?

____

____

____

____

December

Gaining Perspective

Theme

Gaining perspective: Review first semester's progress, using data, observations, and staff, student, and parent perceptions to plan goals for the second term

To Do

Assess first semester progress; plan January inservice based on available student and teacher data

Continue mid-year teacher observations and conferences

Consider which teachers may need closer attention and more observations in the months prior to contract renewal in the spring

Review second semester schedules; make student schedule changes as necessary

Review and revise second semester course assignments and rebalance class loads

Begin planning registration process for next school year

Request mid-year feedback at PTSO or other parent forums, faculty meetings, from student council, and so forth

Other

____

____

Consider This: Insights and Tips From Award-Winning Principals

In December, it's time to regroup. I take advantage of rare quiet time to refocus on the school's mission, follow through with analysis of data and plan for remediation of students in need. I meet with my team leaders to plan an all-school thematic unit for late February and early March to give us a lift during the dreary winter months and that long stretch between winter break and spring break. We plan our second round of half-day grade-level meeting dates, and I look over each teacher's professional development plan for the second semester—with students away and some relatively uninterrupted time, I can study each teacher's goals and update or make revisions based on the progress each one made in the first semester.

Meanwhile, our School Improvement Team meets in December to review our state accreditation plans and make sure we're moving forward on the goals set forth. And I get ready to welcome a new group of student teachers for second semester, some of whom might be prime candidates for vacancies I'll be filling later in the spring.

—Bruce Haddix
2005 NAESP Distinguished Principal
Center Grove Elementary School, Greenwood, IN

I begin planning the end-of-the-year assemblies and programs (for the months of April and May) as soon as possible—no later than January. I ask faculty, staff, and PTSO members to give me the dates for all activities and begin scheduling everything on a calendar that will be mailed out to all parents. It takes a conscious effort to get this mapped out so early, but the advance notice translates to successful events and much better parent participation in your second term events.

—Pam N. Bradley
2005 NAESP Distinguished Principal
Muskogee 7th & 8th Grade Center, Muskogee, OK

If you have the chance between semesters, find a way to celebrate a successful first semester, and the beginning and "fresh start" to the new term! Over the holiday break, write down all of the things that you hoped to do but didn't at the beginning of the year because you got too busy. Now as the real New Year starts, *just do it!* Let your teachers know that you will be in the hallways, in classrooms, doing your observations, meeting with students, and more. In January, you cannot allow yourself any excuses! (And if you go to Florida or Hawaii over Christmas break, don't get a tan—or the community will think you get paid too much!)

Also, be sure to have jumper cables, snow brushes, and shovels in your car for those icy cold afternoons and nights when one of your students, parents, or staff members is stranded. Being prepared for a simple act of kindness, and following through with one, will payoff tenfold in your future, and lay the groundwork for your legacy!

—Gary Lester
2006 NASSP/MetLife Principal of the Year
Thornwood High School, South Holland, IL

Weekly Inspirational Quotes for December

"The true meaning of life is to plant trees, under whose shade you do not expect to sit."

—Nelson Henderson

"Leadership is doing what is right when no one is watching."

—Author unknown

"No problem can withstand the assault of sustained thinking."

—Voltaire

"The truth of the matter is that you always know the right thing to do. The hard part is doing it."

—H. Norman Schwarzkopf

"Success follows trying. Failure also follows trying. Nothing, however, follows nothing. So try!"

—Author unknown

Weekly Reflective Questions for December

Consider the schoolwide goals that you set before the semester and assess your progress. If you've promoted any of the goals to staff and parents publicly, how will you update the school community on your progress, if you haven't done so already? How will you work with your leadership team to evaluate your success and to revise the goals, if necessary, based on emergent needs and your results to date?

____

____

____

____

Reflecting on the school year now halfway completed, consider three to five accomplishments or indicators of progress, profound or subtle, that are satisfying to you, whether they involve teachers, students, support staff, your own performance, or some other outcome related to all the effort and energy you and your staff devoted to children and families so far this year. How can you share and affirm these "victories" with others, as appropriate, among your school community, peer group, supervisors, and your family or friends?

____

____

____

____

Consider the goals you set at the start of the school year for maintaining your own personal vitality. How well have you adhered to the commitments? Are you satisfied with your personal goals at mid-year? What adjustments or additions will benefit you in the second half of the year, as you reaffirm your commitment to nourishing your own family, health, fitness, and leisure needs?

Reflect on your vision for your school, which you may have last taken time to seriously consider back in the summer months. Although progress toward this vision is not to be measured in a matter of months, consider whether events and efforts in the past term align with the long-range direction you've targeted.

Before the first term began, you planned events, programs, and strategies to fuel morale in the school community. Are you satisfied with the effects your efforts have had among your staff, school volunteers, students, and others in the first term? In the second half of the year, when everyone's energy stores are more depleted (including yours!) and inspiration is more important than ever, what new and continuing creative approaches will you use to recognize and motivate your staff?

January

Launching Anew

THEME

Launching anew: Use renewed energy to set the pace for the next term

To Do

Use first semester data to shape inservice training and adjust or develop goals for the spring

Plan one or more major community involvement events for January and February—fine arts night, music concert, science fair, math night, special traditions (e.g., a "Reading Under the Stars" event where community members and local "celebrities" can share their love and zest for reading) that can showcase your school and energize your community during winter and spring

Prepare for and conduct the next round of parent–teacher conference events

Student registration for the next school year

Complete mid-year teacher evaluation conferences and begin developing teacher interventions and growth plans that may be necessary

OTHER

____

____

Consider This: Insights and Tips From Award-Winning Principals

January is when we set up safety nets, determining which students (and sometimes teachers) need additional support. For example, it's mid-year reading evaluation time for our struggling students. We retest students who came in August below grade level to measure their progress. We also use the results to evaluate our remediation programs and our teaching and make adjustments as necessary. We try to incorporate student data in our decisions whenever it's possible—you cannot improve what you don't measure.

—David Montague
2005 NAESP Distinguished Principal
Washington Elementary School, Kennewick, WA

January is a great time to touch base with teachers regarding their professional development goals since it's midway through the school year. I also meet with them to review where they are in their pacing guides so that adjustments can be made if needed prior to our state tests in the spring.

We usually try to schedule our guest authors and other events to make learning fun during the January/February time frame. This helps keep students motivated. Last year, we brought in Marlena Smalls from the Hallelujah Singers during January to integrate the arts into our social studies classes. She taught the students about the Gullah culture through music, and it gave us wonderful curricular themes to integrate instruction and an energy boost that lasted through to spring break.

—Nancy Gregory
2006 NASSP/MetLife Principal of the Year
Blythewood Middle School, Blythewood, SC

During January in the cold Midwest snow and ice, and the short days with little sun, it's a great time to try to pick up the spirits of both students and staff. Be sure that, coming directly from the principal, students and staff know that they are starting the new semester with a "clean slate," and it is great to start the New Year and new semester with some resolutions to be better than ever!

Example for students: Have a "Super Bowl Party" for students who have made it through the championship (first term final exams) successfully! Have a special schedule, and let teachers and students plan activities, by house, by department, by class, or by whatever practical organizational method you use in your building. Let them wear their favorite team jerseys, especially if they are your school colors!

Example for staff: On the Sunday afternoon before the Super Bowl (when there is not a professional football game), have a staff Super Bowl Party where you open the gym, open the swimming pool, have craft activities for the children of staff, and everyone brings food, potluck, to the cafeteria. (We once had an "everyone wins" Olympics competition between children and the staff, during a winter Olympics year.) These sorts of fun activities help break up the doldrums of the long cold winter, getting people out of the house to do something physical. They don't cost much, if anything; just make sure that you clean up well to keep the custodial staff happy (but, of course, include them too, and don't let them work!).

—Gary Lester
2006 NASSP/MetLife Principal of the Year
Thornwood High School, South Holland, IL

Weekly Inspirational Quotes for January

"Courage is not the towering oak that sees storms come and go; it is the fragile blossom that opens in the snow."

—Alice Mackenzie Swain

"Every child is a message that God is not yet discouraged by man."

—Rabindranath Tagore

"The difference between stumbling blocks and stepping stones is how you use them."

—Author unknown

"You are the bows from which your children as living arrows are shot forth."

—Kahlil Gibran

"Education makes people easy to lead, but difficult to drive; easy to govern, but impossible to enslave."

—Henry Peter Brougham

Weekly Reflective Questions for January

If you've kept a reflective log, reread the journal entries you've made in the preceding months. What recurring themes or concerns emerge? How can your reflections assist you in the remainder of this year?

____

____

____

____

The quotation for this month, dealing with stumbling blocks and stepping stones, underscores the importance of attitude. Do you agree with this viewpoint? Would it be useful to share the anecdote with your faculty, parent volunteers, or students, and if so, what real-life examples or stories from your own school community might you use to impart the message?

____

____

____

____

This month's theme is "beginning anew." How can you capitalize on the burst of energy that students and staff bring back to campus after winter break, and sustain it through the "doldrums" in the long weeks stretching out before spring break?

____

____

____

____

Principal David Montague asserts that "you can't improve what you don't measure." Do you agree with him? If so, what accountability systems do you have in place that provide a basis for data-driven decision making, whether with students, staff, or overall school performance? To what extent do your staff, parent association, peers, and central office administration buy into this viewpoint?

____

____

____

____

January is traditionally a time for resolutions—how can you use the colloquial tradition of making resolutions (which can be expressed in fun, creative ways) to frame any changes to or extensions of your schoolwide goals for the staff and school community?

____

____

____

____

February

Maintaining Momentum

Theme

Maintaining momentum: Keeping spirits high and energies focused, while beginning to plan for next year

To Do

The doldrums; teachers can be fatigued and tense in February and March . . .

Mid-quarter reports

Parent conferences

Teacher evaluations

Finish student registration

Begin master schedule planning

Other

Consider This: Insights and Tips From Award-Winning Principals

For that long stretch of time between winter break and spring break, plan an all-school thematic unit that will give the staff and students something fun to look forward to. Ours are usually the first two or three weeks in March, and we have done wonderful things with *The Wizard of Oz* and *Charlie and the Chocolate Factory.* This year, we organized Oh, the Places We'll Go With Dr. Seuss, since the celebration of his birthday was March 2. We transformed the school into Whoville, had a favorite character dress-up day, and then a drive-in movie day to watch *The Cat in the Hat,* and each grade level took a different Seuss book to study. There is no limit to what creative minds can come up with. Makes the dreary winter months a lot more bearable!

—Bruce Haddix
2005 NAESP Distinguished Principal
Center Grove Elementary School, Greenwood, IN

February is a difficult month for many. Sometimes the weather doesn't allow us to get enough sunshine (I'm from Michigan and it leaves the state in November), so I would encourage other leaders to make sure they spend the month building up the morale of the staff. Smile your way through February because the students and staff take their cue from you. Here are some strategies:

Send little notes when you catch someone doing something neat. We use a big stuffed fish. We attach the note with a large safety pin and leave it anonymously in the teacher's classroom. If you get the fish, you keep it for a week and then it is your job to find someone doing something neat and pass it on.

Print out a saying on labels and put them on a miniature candy bar—for instance, buy Peppermint Patties and attach a note saying "Thank you for your commit- 'mint' to the kids!" Give one to everyone or individually as you see the need.

Invite everyone to a staff meeting with a horrible agenda and then have a party instead to celebrate everyone's hard work. Ice cream sundae supplies are cheap and you get a great smile and increased morale.

It is easy to become overwhelmed at this time of year. You have testing, discipline, and no one has a reserve of patience left at this point. Your job is to refill your teachers' banks of positive feelings and patience. They need it. There is a great book titled *If You Don't Feed the Teachers They'll Eat the Students!* This is so true. You must make sure you give your staff the positive affirmation they need to work. You will be amazed at how much it spreads.

—Ronna Steel
2006 NASSP/MetLife Principal of the Year
Union City Middle School, Union City, MI

Heading into the spring, I start to focus on what still needs to happen this year while keeping next year in focus. It's time to "let go" of those things that just did not get off the ground and begin to think about how (or if) we might make them happen next year. It can be hard to let go when we think a program is really important, and equally hard not to start a new initiative that could meet needs identified mid-year, but you really have to choose your battles in the winter and early spring. Staff are fatigued and not that excited about starting new projects at this time of the year.

—Steve Clarke
2005 NASSP/MetLife Principal of the Year
Bellingham High School, Bellingham, WA

Weekly Inspirational Quotes for February

"We miss 100 percent of the shots we don't take."

—Wayne Gretzky

"Our lives begin to end the day we become silent about things that matter."

—Martin Luther King, Jr.

"Courage is not the lack of fear, it is acting in spite of it."

—Mark Twain

"Only those who dare to fail greatly can ever achieve greatly."

—Robert F. Kennedy

Weekly Reflective Questions for February

Taking the cue from the principals who offered suggestions for this month and this time of year—generally finding teachers and students fatigued and low on enthusiasm relative to the excitement of the first months of school or the weeks surrounding the holidays—what creative activities have you planned to boost morale and engagement in your school community during the late winter months?

____

____

____

____

In some schools, February is the time to conclude the formal teacher evaluation process and begin staffing decisions for next year, particularly for teachers who may be placed on growth plans or who may be non-renewed. Aside from these types of intentional faculty attrition, along with retirements, consider your school's turnover rate. Are you satisfied with the level of attrition in your school for the past year? Five years? Ten years? What forces and variables drive teacher turnover at your school and in your community? What strategies do you actively use to minimize turnover at your school?

____

____

____

____

Given the "fatigue factor," professional development activities may be of limited value at this time of year; however, some principals find that engaging teachers to "share out" about effective and innovative practices they use in their classroom is one way to enliven and energize faculty meetings in the late winter months. And other forms of peer-to-peer engagement (like small group book studies) can be a refreshing alternative to principal-driven faculty meetings. Consider whom among your colleagues you might tap to help spark new energy at your meetings through share-outs, book studies, or other collegial catalysts.

In many states, the late winter months initiate the formal ramp-up to district and state standardized testing. How do you help your staff and students temper the importance (and pressures) of test outcomes with a healthful perspective on instructional priorities, including proper nutrition, adequate rest, and a rich and varied instructional "diet" of art, P.E., music—which in turn will benefit test results? Do your behaviors (including explicit and implicit messages you send) add to the stress surrounding testing, or do you intentionally help foster a more relaxed and productive environment for student and teacher achievement? What do you do to inspire success, in the spirit of this month's quotations from Wayne Gretzky, Mark Twain, and Robert F. Kennedy?

March

Looking Both Ways

Theme

Looking both ways: Managing current tasks and priorities while actively planning for next year

To Do

Final preparations for spring standardized testing

Determine staffing needs

Contracts extended to teachers

Planning recruitment for spring and summer

Use current formative data to determine which students are at risk; make sure all students have opportunities for remediation and support

Summative teacher evaluation conferences

Plan for prom, graduation, other end-of-year activities

Build master schedule and master event calendar preliminary drafts for next year

Other

____

____

____

Consider This: Insights and Tips From Award-Winning Principals

This month is always very full. We are involved in state testing during March, and teachers are often busy completing units of work while "worrying" over testing. As principal, I often remind my teachers that testing is important, but it is just one measure of a student's success—a snapshot in time. I reassure the teachers that if they have been promoting high levels of thinking in their classrooms all year and meeting the district and state curricula requirements, students will naturally succeed on test-taking. In addition, in March, we begin to take a final look at students who may need remediation to ensure promotional success for the upcoming year. I begin to finalize the observations of new teachers, and prepare to recommend them for another year of employment. Many times, decisions for teaching new grade levels are begun at this time, too. March is busy, and principals need to stay upbeat through the heavy demands—especially when shades of "the end of the year" are in the air!

—Maria Corso
2005 NAESP Distinguished Principal
Lyncrest School, Fair Lawn, NJ

I try to spend as much time as possible visiting classrooms and doing walkthrough observations during this time. In order to help my teachers feel valued and remind them of the importance of praise and positive relationships, I return to my office after these classroom visits and make positive phone calls to my teachers. I simply call their home phone numbers, knowing that in most cases no one will be home, and then leave them a voicemail on their answering machines. I try to mention some great teaching strategy I have just observed them using, a special way I observed them interact with their students, or any other sincere and specific praise that I can give them. I remind each one that he or she is a great teacher, making differences in the lives of students, and that I appreciate each of them very much. Without exception, the next morning I have smiling, relaxed teachers thanking me for the phone call, which gives me an opportunity to gently remind them that their students need the same kind of positive reinforcement!

—Linda Stroud
2005 NASSP/MetLife Principal of the Year
Greeneville Middle School, Greeneville, TN

Each spring, we host an event we call "Showcase," inviting eighth graders and their parents from feeder schools to campus one evening before they sign up for their classes. The evening starts with a general session for parents that I lead; we discuss how the high school schedule works, what the graduation requirements are, and other basic information. Then the students and parents split up to attend individual sessions all over campus, hosted by various teachers and groups of students. The eighth graders can choose to visit all the sessions they're interested in—they might go to the auditorium to see what our fine arts students and teachers are offering, or see the career and technology program features; there's dance team, drill team, and cheerleaders; our various honor societies and student council; foreign language teachers and students talk about the trips they take each year; there's journalism and yearbook, athletics—lots of different high-interest sessions. And, they're all presented in creative ways and often using technology, happening at various times throughout the evening so kids and parents can visit everything at least once. Our teachers are available to talk to the families all night long. Later in the evening, I present a general session on our pre-AP and pre-IB programs.

The goal of Showcase is to feature all of our interesting signature programs at school, and try to get all of our new high school students connected to at least one program or to a set of students and a teacher, so they are more likely to be engaged and part of the school community from the very beginning. Usually we get almost 100% student and parent attendance. At the end of the evening, we preview and give out the course description handbook, and the eighth graders have three weeks to ask us questions or make individual appointments about any further questions they have before they sign up for classes.

It works really well for us in terms of setting a positive tone among our incoming freshmen, and the eighth graders look forward to the Showcase as a sort of "rite of passage" each year.

—Melinda Reeves
2004 NASSP/MetLife Principal of the Year
Decatur High School, Decatur, TX

Weekly Inspirational Quotes for March

"Our children are watching us live, and what we do shouts louder than anything we say."

—Wilferd A. Peterson

"To believe in the face of utter hopelessness, every article of evidence to the contrary, to ignore apparent catastrophe—what other choice is there? We do it every day. We are so much stronger than we imagine."

—Lance Armstrong

"The aim of education is to teach children how to think, not what to think."

—John Dewey

"If everyone is moving forward together, then success takes care of itself."

—Henry Ford

"Keep away from those who try to belittle your ambitions. Small people always do that, but the really great make you believe that you too can become great."

—Mark Twain

Weekly Reflective Questions for March

The theme this month, "looking both ways," gives a glimpse into the principal's world because at this time of year, not only must school leaders manage the day-to-day operation of the school, they simultaneously need to devote time to planning for next year. Often, that additional planning time is carved from the schedule when the principal would otherwise be visiting classrooms or attending afterschool activities. This is an extraordinarily busy time of year for principals. What do you do differently in the busy spring months to balance your workload and maintain your visibility and effectiveness even while contending with the same fatigue affecting your staff members?

____

____

____

____

If you agree with John Dewey's famous quote, what are you doing to help ensure that "teaching to the test" doesn't completely dominate lesson and unit planning at your school during standardized testing time?

____

____

____

____

Melinda Reeves terms her Showcase a "rite of passage" for her students. What student-centered traditions and events are part of your spring rituals, aside from preparations for testing and anticipation of spring break? What role could a new event play, possibly one coordinated by parent volunteers or your PTSO to minimize the load on your staff, to energize your community around a schoolwide thematic focus this time of year?

____

____

____

____

Whereas our recognition efforts usually focus on students and teachers, many effective principals also acknowledge their classified support staff members and recognize that they too need a boost at this time of the year—particularly because hourly workers in many districts do not have time off during the spring holiday. What do you do to recognize and thank your support staff periodically throughout the year, and especially during the demanding winter and spring months?

____

____

____

____

If like David Montague (January) you've set up "safety nets" for at-risk students, how do you gauge whether the supports are working as you approach the final quarter of the school year? What communication system do you have in place to provide for regular follow-up between the teachers, paraprofessionals, tutors, parents, administrators, counselors, and others involved in the support networks for these students? What role do you take? Is your safety net system effective, and how can it be improved?

____

____

____

____

April

Carrying the Flag

Theme

Carrying the flag: Mobilizing and motivating the school community to pursue and sustain high achievement

To Do

Nationally normed and district tests administered in many states

Teacher recruitment and interviews

Maintaining teacher morale—the end is visible but distant; staff members are tired and stressed due to testing and just the fatigue of the year overall

Final staffing decisions for next year

Teacher evaluation

Continue to refine the master event calendar and master class schedule for next year

Other

Consider This: Insights and Tips From Award-Winning Principals

As the end of the year begins to creep up on us, take some time to reflect upon your accomplishments, your passion for success, and your ability to take time away from your busy schedule. Reflection has to be a conscious effort for most of us, since we're so overscheduled as it is, and self-care is the same way. To keep it all in perspective, each day I hug at least one child!

—Brian McQueen
2005 NAESP Distinguished Principal
Westmoreland Road Elementary School, Whitesboro, NY

The month of April is a tough month. The school year is nearing its end and everyone is trying to make it to the final day. I have found that providing small tokens of appreciation to all staff (cooks, maintenance, clerical, teachers, paraprofessionals) for the job that they have done helps give them their "second wind" so they finish the year strong. I've provided staff with personalized pens, school travel coffee mugs, school portfolio pads, and even small treats in their mailbox. It is also good to be in classrooms and to remain very visible during this time to support the work that is being done in your school. Take time to write at least two thank you notes per day to staff members whom you observe doing things in a positive way that adds to the overall school climate. One must also take care of oneself. We have been working hard and like everyone else, we need to find some time to recharge.

—Dick Jones
2006 NASSP/MetLife Principal of the Year
John Adams Middle School, Rochester, MN

In the spring months, I start thinking about teacher recruitment and filling new and replacement positions for the following school year. The budget is set, retirements, resignations, and non-renewals are sorting themselves out, and it is important to get an early start in a very competitive market.

Hiring the right teachers is the most important part of the job. Holding our own job fair has been very successful for our school. Meeting candidates face-to-face and selling our school is a very important part of the process. Take advantage of this opportunity to sell your school and find the best candidates available. This is also the time of year when motivating both students and staff is essential. We are just starting to get out of the long winter months. Visibility, accessibility, and a positive attitude must be a priority for any administrator at this time. Coming up with motivational ideas for both students and staff is a must. This is always a good time to have a surprise gift or raffle for staff and a fun activity or assembly for students. Get through March and April and it is smooth sailing the rest of the way.

—Jim Elefante
2006 NASSP/MetLife Principal of the Year
Londonderry High School, Londonderry, NH

Weekly Inspirational Quotes for April

"We are what we repeatedly do. Excellence, then, is not an act, but a habit."

—Aristotle

"Excellence is the result of caring more than others think is wise, risking more than others think is safe, dreaming more than others think is practical, and expecting more than others think is possible."

—Author unknown

"In any moment of decision the best thing you can do is the right thing, the next best thing you can do is the wrong thing, and the worst thing you can do is nothing."

—Theodore Roosevelt

"The illiterate of the 21st century will not be those who cannot read and write, but those who cannot learn, unlearn, and relearn."

—Alvin Toffler

"A leader takes people where they want to go. A great leader takes people where they don't necessarily want to go, but ought to be."

—Rosalynn Carter

Weekly Reflective Questions for April

As Brian McQueen notes, it is critical to maintain a perspective in the spring months—the principal's energy level and demeanor "set the weather" at school. Consider your goals for personal nourishment at the start of the year. How well have you maintained your own energy levels and stuck to your aims, whether that entails exercise, family or leisure time, or some other incentive for managing your stressful workload? If you've fallen away from your plans, how can you reestablish them to bolster your reserves and thereby help your school community finish strong?

____

____

____

____

____

Jim Elefante asserts that teacher selection is the most important aspect of the principal's work. Hiring great teachers and helping them improve through your evaluation process are two critical variables in student achievement that principals can control. How much time and energy do you dedicate to teacher recruitment, selection, and development? Are you successful in consistently hiring excellent teachers? Do you have peers who might share suggestions and tricks of the trade for improving your process or results?

____

____

____

____

____

This month's theme is "carrying the flag." The anonymous quotation about excellence relates to the need for school leaders to inspire extraordinary commitment and sacrifice, especially moving through the last months of the school year. What are you doing to motivate your staff, students, and parent volunteers to extract their best efforts and help maintain their sense of humor (and yours)?

____

____

____

____

____

Developing the master course schedule and event calendar in some schools is similar to a game of chess. Often, creative solutions emerge when fresh sets of eyes consider the various challenges implicit in developing these complex systems. In addition, having broader participation helps to communicate the rationale for the difficult scheduling decisions that school leaders occasionally have to make. Have any of your staff members, besides the registrar, been tapped to assist with scheduling in the past? Assuming it would be beneficial given the dynamics of scheduling at your school, who might you consider to participate at some level in the process?

____

____

____

____

____

Occasionally, opportunities present themselves to publicly promote your school and highlight the qualities of your students, staff, programs, and community that make your school appealing. This is certainly true during teacher recruitment and in meetings with parents; though often, you have only a short time to convey the positive attributes, and you need to do it in a compelling, memorable way. An "elevator speech" is a concise and engaging summary used in sales and marketing (so-named because it can be delivered in the time it takes to ride up an elevator with a prospective client). What unique, exciting aspects of your school would you include in your elevator speech when you want to "sell" your school to an individual or audience in a very limited time frame?

____

____

____

____

____

May

Finishing Strong

Theme

Finishing strong: Keeping colleagues and students motivated, meaningfully engaged, and striving down to the wire

To Do

A month of testing in some states, and the end of school in others

Finish strong: Plan projects and high-interest activities that allow students to integrate learning across disciplines, and insist that quality instruction take place through the final day of classes

Engage in teacher recruitment and schedule interviews while the candidate pool is deepest as the hiring process goes into full swing

Finish teacher evaluations

Make summer plans for renovation and remodeling

Plan with staff for summer curriculum work

Plan for summer remediation programs and getting students signed up

Continue refining master activities calendar and course schedule for next year

Other

Consider This: Insights and Tips From Award-Winning Principals

May is a productive month for me—I try to focus a lot of my remaining energy to make progress in wrapping up the year while getting a good start on planning for next year. I begin work on all the end-of-year celebrations—still a month away, but the month will fly!—teachers retiring, fifth-grade graduation, our Festival of the Arts and student talent show, our annual charity walk activities, textbook inventories and ordering, and developing a final calendar for the fall with registration, open houses, and so forth, to go home with the students during the final week of school. I end the year with a positive final correspondence to parents, focusing on a "celebration" theme—all the things to celebrate from the past year about which they can be proud of the students and school. If I have a productive May, it makes June much easier and helps ensure I'll enjoy a much-needed block of time for myself in July.

—Bruce Haddix
2005 NAESP Distinguished Principal
Center Grove Elementary School, Greenwood, IN

The end of the school year is always exhausting and full of activities. Teachers and support staff need to know how much their efforts were appreciated throughout the year. I make sure to do an appreciation activity or luncheon to honor them. One of my favorites is an "Oscar Mayer Winners" assembly in which teachers receive funny gifts based on events of that school year. We have music, food, and funny tokens or items to give teachers. At this time of year, I also get input from the entire school community as to how to improve for next year. I survey the staff, community, and students—or host meetings to find out what worked, and what didn't, and solicit their suggestions for making things better for the upcoming school year. Their ideas often prove to be quite creative and so much better than my own! I then use the input to plan for the following year. Finally, if we're organizing a back-to-school night for the following year, we do an early mail out to parents with the dates and information so parents can put the information on their calendars early.

—Pam N. Bradley
2005 NAESP Distinguished Principal
Muskogee 7th & 8th Grade Center, Muskogee, OK

At the end of the year it can be very difficult to keep students and teachers focused on final exams. They are all looking forward to summer vacation. As a principal, it is imperative that we get into classrooms at this time of year, even though we have a very hectic schedule, to be sure that solid instruction is still taking place and solid review is underway to prepare the students for those exams. If you have the ability to adjust scheduling of exams, shorter blocks spread over a few days seem to work better at our school this time of year.

I remind myself that graduation is the culmination of thirteen years of education, a time to celebrate and rejoice for students, teachers, families, and friends. This is one celebration that we want to get right! I create a checklist that includes every necessary detail and the names of those people who have various responsibilities to see that everything is ready to go on this special day. I make certain that whoever is reading students' names has the correct pronunciation. Every parent, grandparent, aunt, and uncle wants to hear the family name read correctly. Also, I make sure to include some fun! Graduation is a celebration and should not be a solemn occasion.

—Todd Wolverton
2005 NASSP/MetLife Principal of the Year
Creston High School, Creston, IA

Weekly Inspirational Quotes for May

"Failure is an attitude, not an outcome."

—Harvey Mackay

"Live as if you were to die tomorrow. Learn as if you were to live forever."

—Mahatma Gandhi

"A mind stretched to a new idea, never goes back to its original dimensions."

—Oliver Wendell Holmes

"Be bold. If you're going to make an error, make it a doozy, and don't be afraid to hit the ball."

—Billie Jean King

"The roots of education are bitter, but the fruit is sweet."

—Aristotle

WEEKLY REFLECTIVE QUESTIONS FOR MAY

As Todd Wolverton points out, visibility is critical to maintaining a productive school climate as the end of the school year approaches. What do you do to stay visible across your campus, even as teacher recruitment and evaluation and other end-of-year obligations add to your workload?

Sometimes principals see a spike in conduct problems as the end of the school year approaches, especially in the secondary grades. What do you and your staff members do proactively to help mitigate this phenomenon before problems occur?

How are retiring and departing teachers honored at your school? Do you have a memorable way to commemorate their service? What do your peers at other area schools do that is special or unique?

Some secondary schools are prone to the unfortunate "tradition" of ending the year with a student prank. Do your students engage in this sort of behavior? If so, can you investigate ways other school leaders have found to terminate, confound, minimize, or negotiate away this frustrating and potentially dangerous year-end problem?

____

____

____

____

What strategies do you use to ensure that meaningful learning experiences continue through the final days of the school year, whether this amounts to policies, practices, or just expectations communicated to the staff and students? How do you monitor the quality of instruction as the end of the school year nears?

____

____

____

____

June

Celebrating, Commemorating, and Looking Forward

Theme

Celebrating, commemorating, and looking forward: Bring the school year to a close and engage in active planning for the upcoming fall term

To Do

Commencement and other transition ceremonies

Staff socials, recognition events

Complete hiring, plan for next school year, analyze data, meet with district administrators

Modify master course schedule as needed

Review previous year's data and issues

Revise student and staff handbooks

Meet with the administrative, staff support, teacher leaders, and counseling teams to review, plan, and improve

Plan and conduct end-of-year leadership team meeting and schedule summer meetings

Begin planning start-of-school inservice training based on student achievement data and emergent needs from the previous year

Other

____

____

Consider This: Insights and Tips From Award-Winning Principals

After the kids and teachers leave, and before a July respite, I pick up some great postcards and send each teacher one during their summer recess. I like to send ones of the local areas or one from National Geographic, Smithsonian, or other organization that features national monuments. Even better, if I am at a convention or training, I add a sentence like: "I am attending the University of Iowa math conference and was thinking about the great polygon activity I saw in your class last spring." I include a wish for relaxation and expectations for the upcoming school year. I always do this, and always get great feedback and comments.

I use this quiet time to catch up on tickler items. I put all significant birthdays on reminder systems, and address a card for each teacher in the summer. Then, since the actual birth date is penciled at the top left, I am ready to put it in their mailbox on their day. Another trick I've learned about this time: I know that it is easier to e-mail an invitation to a teacher to sponsor or lead a program or activity when they are rested in June or July rather than when they are frazzled in May!

I also use this time to get caught up on professional reading. I look over all the Web sites for professional organizations, in addition to that pile of unread journals . . .

I write letters of thanks to those on the periphery: contractors, custodial people, helpful parents—some on letterhead for their work file or handwritten notes for special parent support. In my notes and letters I am specific about what I appreciated and leave an invitation to stay involved in the future. For example, "Thank you for all of your kind efforts in support of our school feeding program. You were always interested in resolving issues and improving quality and service for our students. I so look forward to partnering with you again in the fall, and know that the challenge with our new meal crediting system is nothing that we will not be able to conquer together!"

I also use this time to plan a welcome back for teachers. The best one recently centered on a Greek theme: Big Fat Greek Welcome Back party with Greek food, the soundtrack from Zorba and other "Greek themed" movies, trivia, and a loaded squirt gun for each of the 111 staff members!

I plan something significant and special for any new staff member, and set a time to meet before we all crowd in for a group welcome during the rush of orientation.

I walk the floors of the school and in the rooms once per week with the teachers and students gone. When the place is quiet, you can get a feel for what needs to be done, and with time away from kids and a full staff, some good ideas may evolve.

I go to the school library and read one children's book a week that I had not read before. I do that during a break in the day—and summer means actually getting a lunch break!

—Melissa Klopfer
2005 NAESP Distinguished Principal
Aviano Elementary School Department of
Defense Education Activity (DoDEA), Italy

During a busy summer of work for the custodial crew, we have a tradition of holding a steak barbecue during their lunchtime in the courtyard. The vice principal and I grill steaks and have baked potatoes with all of the trimmings. It is a nice way to thank them for all of their work throughout the summer.

—Mike Scott
2004 NASSP/MetLife Principal of the Year
Poynter Middle School, Hillsboro, OR

For June, I devise an advance calendar/timeline to the end of next year that includes all the to-do tasks and regularly scheduled events, noting any changes I want to make based on how this year went. Then, I plot out major goals for next year. I identify the areas where I must have staff input for the start-of-school agenda, and then I place time for next year's forward thinking activities on the calendar. By doing so, and involving teachers in the process and sharing the evolving calendar with them throughout the last month of school, it requires staff to be forward thinking as well, and prevents them from being "shocked with the changes" when they come back after the summer. I make sure to complete this exercise before the end of June when the teachers disappear.

—Gary Lester
2006 NASSP/MetLife Principal of the Year
Thornwood High School, South Holland, IL

Weekly Inspirational Quotes for June

"Those who dare to teach must never cease to learn."

—Socrates

"Never doubt that a small group of people can change the world. Indeed, it's the only thing that ever does."

—Margaret Mead

"Optimism is the faith that leads to achievement. Nothing can be done without hope and confidence."

—Helen Keller

"The real voyage of discovery consists not in making new landscapes but in having new eyes."

—Marcel Proust

"Teamwork is the fuel that allows common people to attain uncommon results."

—Andrew Carnegie

Weekly Reflective Questions for June

What three specific actions can you do for yourself this summer that will help you recharge for next year?

____

____

____

____

____

Melissa Klopfer's suggestions reflect her very productive use of the precious additional time school leaders enjoy during the summer months, starting after the teachers leave in most districts in June. Do you have a plan for using your summer work time most effectively? The summer months will fly past—have you begun listing and prioritizing the tasks or objectives you intend to address in the weeks ahead?

School leaders model the learning they expect to see in children and teachers each year. Reflect on what you've learned this year, how you've grown, and where you may have reached or fell short of the goals you set for yourself before the school year started. Would it be beneficial to share any of this with your staff in the fall?

What major challenges emerged or intensified this year and kept you awake at night? How will you address the concerns next year, and how in the future might you avoid the same circumstances happening again?"

Based on the school year that's finished or nearly complete, and while it's still relatively fresh in your mind, begin thinking about three personal or professional goals you wish to set for yourself in the year ahead. How will you measure your success?

____

____

____

____

____

July

Reflecting, Affirming, and Rejuvenating

Theme

Reflecting, affirming, and rejuvenating: Make time to gain perspective and reenergize while attending to any remaining planning and staffing needs, and shift to a forward focus

To Do

Complete hiring

Continue to plan for next school year using available data

Read, reflect, grow, be encouraged, play, exercise, seek adventure, gain perspective, unplug

Other

____

____

____

____

____

____

Consider This: Insights and Tips From Award-Winning Principals

I live by the three R's for July. Pursue *restful* activities to get the body ready for another year, take *responsibility* for making sure excellent staff are hired and in place, and *ripen* your mind with new ideas to inspire students, staff, and parents to be the best they can be.

—Suzanne E. Smith
2005 NAESP Distinguished Principal
Gertrude Walker Elementary School, Garden City, KS

July is the month in which we, as principals, must take time to reflect, replenish, and renew ourselves personally and professionally. Past victories and defeats must be viewed as catalysts to strengthen and reinvigorate our spiritual lives and dreams as well as to sustain and energize our professional vision. We must give courage to our commitment to be lifted so that we may lift others. In other words: take the kids to the beach, read a noneducational book, eat a real lunch, sleep for more than four hours a night, and dream what some might consider "that impossible dream!"

—Sharon Byrdsong
2005 NASSP Principal of the Year
Azalea Gardens Middle School, Norfolk, VA

In July, I hold an annual administrative retreat, including my assistant principals and counselors. It doesn't cost a lot—last year we went to a lake and stayed at cabins. We work hard through an agenda I prepare, planning our fall inservice training, making all the changes to our handbooks. We have time for lots of talking and a chance to work together closely for a sustained time, which is so hard to do during the school year with all the distractions. We find it to be extremely high quality time.

At the retreat, we plan a "theme" for the year. (For example, last year we moved out of a dilapidated building into a new, modern facility, and we developed the next year's theme as "extreme makeover" with "building blocks for learning.") We map out all the different duties, finalize staffing and assignments, and be sure that everyone on the leadership team knows what needs to be done when we reassemble for the start of school.

—Melinda Reeves
2004 NASSP/MetLife Principal of the Year
Decatur High School, Decatur, TX

Weekly Inspirational Quotes for July

"We must be the change we wish to see."

—Mahatma Gandhi

"I have believed as many as six impossible things before breakfast."

—Lewis Carroll

"Use your eyes as if tomorrow you would be stricken blind . . . Hear the music of voices, the song of the bird, the mighty strains of an orchestra, as if you would be stricken deaf tomorrow. Touch each object as if tomorrow your tactile sense would fail. Smell the perfume of the flowers, taste with relish each morsel, as if tomorrow you could never smell and taste again. Make the most of every sense; glory in all the facets of pleasure and beauty which the world reveals to you."

—Helen Keller

"We are now at a point where we must educate our children in what no one knew yesterday, and prepare our schools for what no one knows yet."

—Margaret Meade

"A leader is best when people barely know he exists. When his work is done, his aim fulfilled, they will say: We did it ourselves."

—Lao-Tzu

Weekly Reflective Questions for July

This month's theme is "reflecting, affirming, and rejuvenating." Take a moment to consider what elements in your life—professionally and personally—are your sources of nourishment. To what extent have you made these individuals, activities, interactions, and hobbies part of your routine to "rejuvenate" during the school year and now, in the relative quiet of the summer? Considering that you are most able to lead when you're most energized and healthful, how can you incorporate more of what sustains you into your days, nights, and weekends next year—starting *now?*

____

____

____

____

Develop a long-range vision for your school—where do you want to lead your community in the next three to five years? List several areas of the school's operations, programs, or personnel you'd like to improve, along with strategies to get there, timelines, and specific indicators of progress that will be your measures of success.

____

____

____

____

So often, school leaders must focus their attention on the endless problems and concerns that define day-to-day life in many schools. Reflecting on the school year behind you now, as you did in December, consider five accomplishments or indicators of progress, profound or subtle, that bring you satisfaction, whether they involve teachers, students, support staff, your own performance, or some other outcome related to all the effort and energy you and your staff devoted to children and families this year. How do you share and celebrate these victories with others, as appropriate, among your school community, peer group, supervisors, and your family or friends?

Margaret Mead's famous line about the small group that changes the world applies to organizations like schools, too. Who among your staff constitute your "small group," the early adapters who embrace innovative changes and implement new ideas? Being sensitive to their relationships with their peers, how can you leverage their support so that their advocacy for the positive changes you propose becomes contagious (rather than divisive) among the less-enthusiastic staff members?

Review your orientation plan for new and returning faculty. Do you meet their needs each year? What's missing? Do you invite teachers to formally assess their orientation experience so you can continually improve it? Have you surveyed your peers to explore other creative, engaging, motivational strategies for welcoming your staff back, orienting new staff, and preparing for the year ahead?

Resources

WAYS TO . . .

Here are some additional ideas to support the suggestions presented in the book.

Ways to Get Parents Involved

It's usually easier to engage parents of younger students—elementary and middle schoolers—than it is parents of high schoolers. To maximize your opportunity for attracting the most parents to an event, you need to schedule the meeting or forum at times that are most convenient for them. Some principals host coffees or less-formal gatherings at different times of the day, on multiple days, and even at different locations depending on the geographic range of their attendance zones.

Interestingly, some principals find that offering food (or sometimes pot luck) increases participation; this can be tied to cultural aspects of a parent community, and learning about the different habits and beliefs of one's constituents can provide other "lures" (and taboos) to maximize parent participation. But food, music, visuals like footage of children participating in school events, and other "comforts" increase a sense of belonging for parents that makes attending school events more appealing.

One of the most effective strategies I've found for engaging less-active parents, and this works particularly well as a lead-in to a conversation about a conduct problem, is to appeal to the parent for assistance. "We want your child to be successful; you know her (or him) better than any of us, and I want to work with you to help her excel, improve, and work through this problem," and so forth. Parents want to feel successful raising their children; and by valuing parents especially during times of crisis or uncertainty, you can build relationships and diffuse tensions, which will help increase the chances of gaining their loyalty and support.

Just as teachers sometimes enlist reluctant learners or restless, unruly students as aides or helpers to channel their energy productively, some principals find this is the best way to mobilize parents who might not be supportive of your administration. It's a bit dramatic in the context of running a school, but the old adage of "keeping your enemies close" rings true for me. There's nothing more rewarding than inviting a naysayer parent onto an important committee and observing his transition over time as he begins to understand the complexity of your decision-making responsibilities and appreciate the great staff and parent volunteers who serve the school.

Ways to Set Aside Time for Professional Development

Principals can build more time for professional development in their schools by using three effective strategies:

1. Lengthen the calendar year to create more professional development days (not usually an easy option in many large urban or suburban systems).
2. Integrate opportunities to share effective strategies and innovations into your faculty meetings. This is especially effective if teachers deliver the ideas to other teachers.
3. "Bank" minutes from the daily schedule—by trimming a minute or two from lunch, starting a minute or two earlier each day, and ending school a few minutes later, you can accumulate 45 minutes or more each week to build in time for weekly collaborative planning and training sessions, without causing much disruption to the daily schedule.

Whichever strategy you choose, it's important to conduct professional development within the regular workday whenever possible. For starters, it's more effective to bring teachers together when they're not fatigued at the end of the day, thinking about their lessons in the early morning, or wishing they were with family on the weekend. And it values teachers as professionals not to take away from time they could use in other ways. Also, many principals find that "one-shot wonders"—professional trainings delivered in one session at the start of the year, usually, and then not followed up on in subsequent sessions—are rarely as effective as periodically revisiting and reflecting on the new learnings throughout the school year.

Ways to Get out of the Front Office

There's no silver bullet for this one. There are always, *always* other pressing tasks at hand, but if it's important to you to maintain a presence, knowing what's happening in your school, and making sure your teachers know you value what they're doing, you just have to make it happen. Some principals find it useful to actually schedule time to make informal classroom drop-ins (what I call "dipsticking") every week; then, make sure everyone in the office understands that this time is sacrosanct (as much as possible anyway). In my experience, everyone (including parents and central office administrators) appreciate principals who make instructional supervision their top priority. In addition, studies demonstrate that staff notice where the principal spends her time—school leaders who appear to "drift" from the classrooms, teachers, and students, and become less involved in the daily life of the school, lose credibility and risk impacting morale if they're too busy to spend time in classrooms.

Ways to Deal With Change in Schools

Teachers generally are not risk takers, and they like stability. (If they took risks and sought professional thrills, they'd have gravitated to stockbroking or venture capitalism!) Consequently, they can be averse to change—especially since our profession is so saturated with trends that seem to come and go and recycle over time.

Again, there are no magic solutions to implementing change in schools, but principals are wise to consider the following general observations:

Be careful about trying to implement too many changes at once. Not only can it be exhausting for staff (and for you) to manage multiple initiatives, if you have too many variables, and you experience success (or failure), you may not know which change was responsible!

Try to start small if you can. Enlist a small cadre of teachers who can be "early adapters," enthusiastic about experimenting and likely to put good effort into the new approach. Often, if a few teachers experience success, especially if the group includes one or more of the informal leaders among the staff, other teachers will be compelled to sign on. Successful changes are contagious that way.

Take time to make sure your constituents understand the change you're proposing before you implement it. Rob Evans, a noted lecturer on school change, addressed my faculty, staff, and administrators when he visited our school in 2004 to help us work through a major instructional change initiative. He told us that teachers deserve to know (a) *why* we're making a change, (b) *what* we're changing to, and (c) *how* we're going to get there.

Change can happen in schools autocratically, but you risk sustainability (i.e., how likely is it that the changes you impose will survive your tenure?). Change can also come about democratically, but it can take a very long time to reach a consensus. Inviting teachers and other constituents to participate in the process and provide input, with the explicit understanding that you as principal need to make the final decision, is an approach that many principals today find effective.

Ways to Balance Personal Time Against Work Commitments

Strategies for time management vary as widely as personalities of the principals themselves. But a common thread that runs through the accounts of veteran principals is that we need to be intentional about making time for ourselves, for our fitness and personal nourishment, for our families and friends, because if we don't, the job will consume us (or unhealthful habits will). Joining a professional organization like NAESP or NASSP provides access to excellent resources to help you from trying to invent every wheel yourself. Attending conferences affords a chance to relax, refresh, change pace, and build a support system—nobody understands and can help with a stressful issue better than a fellow principal, and it's very stimulating to be surrounded by colleagues who are all contending with very similar challenges. Regular exercise offers wonderful benefits for stress release and emotional balance, accompanied by good nutrition and sufficient sleep. If you don't develop strategies to make time for your own wellness, though, the job will certainly not make such time abundant. And if you don't take care of yourself because you're spending all your time on work, your work performance will eventually start to suffer. Nobody will fault you for occasionally taking a walk during lunch or after the students leave campus; but they'll be less forgiving if you're often out ill, or you're frequently grumpy, or you exhibit other symptoms of stress that accompany a life out of balance. Take care of yourself so you can best take care of others!

MAKING TIME TO REFLECT

When I shared my idea for this book with sitting and former school leaders, the ubiquitous response was something like, "That's a great idea—it took me years to recognize the importance of reflection. I just had no time early on!"

Personally, I'm not sure there's any more time in my day now, after a decade as a school leader; but several years ago a mentor made an indelible impression on me by saying, simply and persuasively, "if it's important, you make time for it." So, now I reflect.

This section's heading is a bit of a misnomer. There is no single "way" to make time to practice reflection. Some principals use their drive to and from work to unwind and process the day. Others need to write notes or log journal entries to put it in perspective. Some of us have spouses or partners who tolerate (and even encourage) venting and vetting issues and concerns. (And some of us have jeopardized our relationships by saturating our significant others with our reflections and problems.)

Personally, I've found a very effective combination of exercise and reflection in the early morning before my family is awake. Never in my first years as an administrator would I have opted to awaken before daylight to exercise or to process whatever kept me awake the night before, but now, that precious hour or so in the predawn darkness is a daily catalyst that I know helps sustain my energy levels and keep me mentally and emotionally balanced. I still don't always jump out of bed to get serious and sweaty; but the dual satisfaction of finishing a workout and thinking through a troublesome issue, or occasionally enjoying the comparative luxury of reading a journal article "for fun" on the exercise bike—these morning activities have become addictive for me and for peers I know who, like me, strive to balance an unrelenting job with family time and personal fitness goals.

The main thing is creating the context for reflection that works for you. The method and particular mode for reflection depend on your preferences, life circumstances, and disposition. If it's important, you'll make the time! I promise you'll benefit from the habit of reflection, and I hope this book can be useful in getting there.